NORTH AMERICAN ANIMALS

Gray Wolves

by Christina Leaf

BELLWETHER MEDIA · MINNEAPOLIS, MN

Note to Librarians, Teachers, and Parents:

Blastoff! Readers are carefully developed by literacy experts and combine standards-based content with developmentally appropriate text.

Level 1 provides the most support through repetition of high-frequency words, light text, predictable sentence patterns, and strong visual support.

Level 2 offers early readers a bit more challenge through varied simple sentences, increased text load, and less repetition of high-frequency words.

Level 3 advances early-fluent readers toward fluency through increased text and concept load, less reliance on visuals, longer sentences, and more literary language.

Level 4 builds reading stamina by providing more text per page, increased use of punctuation, greater variation in sentence patterns, and increasingly challenging vocabulary.

Level 5 encourages children to move from "learning to read" to "reading to learn" by providing even more text, varied writing styles, and less familiar topics.

Whichever book is right for your reader, Blastoff! Readers are the perfect books to build confidence and encourage a love of reading that will last a lifetime!

This edition first published in 2015 by Bellwether Media, Inc.

No part of this publication may be reproduced in whole or in part without written permission of the publisher. For information regarding permission, write to Bellwether Media, Inc., Attention: Permissions Department, 5357 Penn Avenue South, Minneapolis, MN 55419.

Library of Congress Cataloging-in-Publication Data

Leaf, Christina, author.
  Gray Wolves / by Christina Leaf.
    pages cm. – (Blastoff! Readers. North American Animals)
  Includes bibliographical references and index
  Summary: "Simple text and full-color photography introduce beginning readers to gray wolves. Developed by literacy experts for students in kindergarten through third grade"– Provided by publisher.
  Audience: Ages 5-8.
  Audience: K to Grade 3.
  ISBN 978-1-62617-188-6 (hardcover : alk. paper)
  1. Gray wolf–Juvenile literature. I. Title.
  QL737.C22L435 2015
  599.773–dc23
                                                    2014042323

Table of
Contents

What Are Gray Wolves?

Gray wolves are powerful **predators**. These **mammals** once hunted across most of North America.

In the Wild

N
W — E
S

gray wolf range = ▢

conservation status: least concern
(endangered in some regions)

Extinct

Extinct in
the Wild

Critically
Endangered

Endangered

Vulnerable

Near
Threatened

Least
Concern

Today, they roam around Canada, eastern Greenland, and northern areas of the United States.

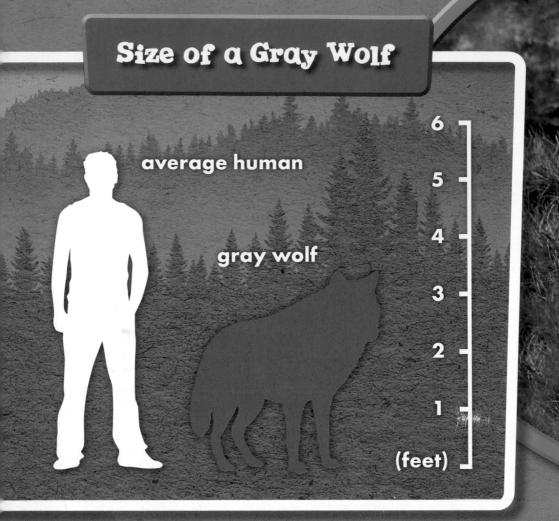

Size of a Gray Wolf

average human

gray wolf

6
5
4
3
2
1
(feet)

Gray wolves belong to the dog family. They have extra long legs and big paws.

They can be up to 6.5 feet (2 meters) long from nose to tail tip.

Identify a Gray Wolf

bushy tail with black tip

rounded ears

sharp teeth

These wild dogs are comfortable in almost any **habitat**. Their **territories** may include forests, **tundra**, grasslands, or mountains.

Thick fur keeps gray wolves warm in cold areas. Its gray color gives the animals their name. However, gray wolves can have black, brown, or even white fur.

Gray wolves live in family groups called **packs**. A pack usually has between four and nine wolves.

A **dominant** pair leads the
pack. They are often the parents
of the other wolves.

On the Hunt

A pack works together to find food. The hunt starts with a **howl**.

This tells the pack to gather.
It also warns other wolves to
stay away from their territory.

These **carnivores** look for hoofed animals such as deer and elk.

moose

elk

American bison

white-tailed deer

snowshoe hares

caribou

As a pack, gray wolves can take down **prey** much bigger than themselves.

The wolves feast after a successful hunt. They eat enough to survive until their next catch.

They do not always catch their prey. This means they do not eat every day.

The dominant female gives birth in spring. She usually has four to seven **pups** in her litter. Pups are born blind and deaf. Mom feeds her helpless babies and carries them in her mouth.

Baby Facts

Name for babies:	pups
Size of litter:	4 to 7 pups
Length of pregnancy:	60 to 63 days
Time spent with mom:	1 to 3 years

Soon the pups run and play-fight outside of their **den**. They are hunting by winter.

After one to three years, they may leave to start their own pack!

Glossary

carnivores—animals that only eat meat

den—a sheltered place; wolf pups are raised in dens.

dominant—commanding or leading

habitat—a land area with certain types of plants, animals, and weather

howl—a loud, long cry

mammals—warm-blooded animals that have backbones and feed their young milk

packs—groups of wolves that live and hunt together

predators—animals that hunt other animals for food

prey—animals that are hunted by other animals for food

pups—baby wolves

territories—land areas where animal groups live

tundra—dry land where the ground is frozen year-round

To Learn More

AT THE LIBRARY

Brandenburg, Jim and Judy. *Face to Face With Wolves*. Washington, D.C.: National Geographic, 2008.

George, Jean Craighead. *The Wolves Are Back*. New York, N.Y.: Dutton Children's Books, 2008.

Marsh, Laura. *Wolves*. Washington, D.C.: National Geographic, 2012.

ON THE WEB

Learning more about gray wolves is as easy as 1, 2, 3.

1. Go to www.factsurfer.com.

2. Enter "gray wolves" into the search box.

3. Click the "Surf" button and you will see a list of related web sites.

With factsurfer.com, finding more information is just a click away.

Index